GIVE A
MAGIC SHOW!

GIVE A
MAGIC SHOW!

BY

Burton and Rita Marks

illustrated by Don Madden

Lothrop, Lee & Shepard Co.
A Division of
William Morrow & Co., Inc. • New York

Text copyright © 1977 by Burton Marks and Rita Marks
Illustrations copyright © 1977 by Don Madden

1   2   3   4   5   6   7   8   9   10

Library of Congress Cataloging in Publication Data

Marks, Burton.
  Give a magic show!
  Includes index.
  SUMMARY: Instructions for performing seventeen magic tricks, with directions for making a costume, wand, hat, and rabbit.
  1. Conjuring—Juvenile literature.   [1. Magic tricks]
I. Marks, Rita, joint author.   II. Madden, Don, 1927–   III. Title.
GV1548.M35   793.8   77-5436
ISBN 0-688-41819-8
ISBN 0-688-51819-2 lib. bdg.

To Craig and Wayne

CONTENTS

"Quiet, everyone. The magic show is about to begin." The curtain opens. The stage is dark. Then from out of nowhere the Magician appears—waving a magic wand. Suddenly wonderful things begin to happen. A rabbit comes out of a hat. A handkerchief appears in an empty box. A wand rises in a bottle. The stage becomes a place of mystery and magic. At the end of the show, to everyone's surprise, the Magician vanishes into thin air! The audience laughs and applauds. What a wonderful magic show!

Would you like to pull a rabbit out of a hat, make a wand rise in a bottle, or vanish into thin air? This book tells you how. These tricks look very mystifying, but they are really easy to do. When you learn how to do them, and others, too, you can give your own magic show and fool your friends. But watch out . . . you may be fooled, too!

9

SETTING
THE STAGE

Your theater can be almost any large room—at home, at a club meeting hall, or even at school. Set up your stage at one end of the room, so that no one can walk behind you. Line up chairs for the audience in front of the stage. You will need two small tables—card tables will do—one on each side of the stage. Cover each table with a cloth. Arrange your equipment on one table and perform your tricks at the other. If your stage is in a basement or garage, you might stretch a clothes line across it to hold a curtain. The curtain can be an old sheet. Pin it to the clothes line so that it will slide along the top. Pull the curtain to one side when the show begins.

Make a poster to advertise the show. It might look like this:

MAKING A COSTUME

Wear a costume for the show. It can be a simple one that you make yourself. You will need two strips of cotton material—each about 15 inches wide and 4½ feet long. They can be any color, but red or gold is best. You'll use one strip for a turban and the other for a sash.

To make the turban, place the cloth on your head like this (Figure 1).

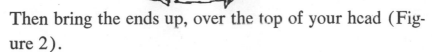

Then bring the ends up, over the top of your head (Figure 2).

Cross the ends in front and tuck them in the back (Figure 3).

3.

To make the sash, tie the other strip around your waist and let the ends hang to one side (Figure 4).

4.

You can also make a cape. It can be a dramatic color like black or bright red. Make it out of crepe paper or shiny cloth. Use a bath towel for a pattern. Place it on the cloth or the crepe paper and carefully cut around it.

Gather the cape at the top and wrap it around your shoulders. Fasten it in front with a costume jewelry pin, if you have one, or a safety pin. To complete your costume wear a long-sleeved white shirt or blouse and dark slacks or skirt, with pockets. (Pockets will be important.)

Put on your costume and look in the mirror. Behold a magician standing before you!

PLANNING THE PROGRAM

First, read each trick carefully. Then choose the ones that you like best and practice them in front of a mirror. Talk while you do them—that's important. Say funny things that will make people laugh. Practice the tricks over and over again until you can do them smoothly. Show them to members of your family. If you are doing something not quite right, they can help you. When you think you are good enough you can plan a show for your friends.

For your first show choose five or six of your best tricks. Then arrange them into an interesting program. Start off with a short trick—one that will surprise the audience quickly and make a good first impression. Your very best trick should be saved for last. A good program should have a variety of tricks. It should be exciting and full of surprises. Here are two sample programs that you can follow.

#1 (A short program)
1. *The Rabbit in the Hat*
2. *The Rising Wand*
3. *The Changing Bag*
4. *The Invisible Penny*

5. *The Loop and Cord Mystery*
6. *The Magic Cone*

#2 (A longer program that you might use for your second or third show.)
1. *The Knotty Handkerchiefs*
2. *The Vanishing Wand*
3. *The Phantom Dime*
4. *The Magic Water Trick*
5. *The Spooky Matchbox*
6. *The Broken Match Mystery*
7. *The Funny Paper Loops*
8. *Now You See Me—Now You Don't!*

Have a rehearsal before the show. Do each trick on your program as if it were the real show. Pretend that the audience is in front of you—listening to you and watching every move that you make. For each trick, practice exactly what you are going to do and exactly what you are going to say. Then you know it will be a good show.

SHOWTIME!

The audience is seated. Everything is ready. Suddenly the curtain opens and you are in the middle of the stage, in your turban, sash and cape. If your hands are shaky and your knees a little wobbly, don't worry. That's what performers call "stage fright" or "opening-night jitters." After you have performed your first trick and it is a big success, the jitters will disappear . . . . just like magic.

Smile while you perform. Relax and be yourself. Let the audience know you are having fun. Then they will relax and have fun, too.

Take your time with each trick. Be sure the audience can follow what you are doing. But when a trick is over, move quickly to another one. Don't give the audience time to think about how the trick was done.

If a trick fails, don't be upset. Instead, make a joke of it. Pretend that it didn't work because you said the wrong magic words. Then start a new trick right away.

At the end of the show thank your audience for coming and say, "I hope that you enjoyed the show." Then take a bow and vanish into thin air!

SIMPLE SLEIGHT OF HAND TRICKS

Your fingers will help you to do these tricks. They will make secret moves that no one will see. The tricks are easy to do but you must practice them. Practice each move until it looks smooth and natural. Stand in front of a mirror to see what the audience sees.

THE BALANCING GLASS———————————————————★
The magician does a balancing act.

The Trick:

Hold up a playing card and a glass and—*Presto!*—balance the glass on the edge of the card. Be careful—the glass might fall if you don't know the secret.

18

How to Do It:

For safety, use a clear plastic glass that looks like a real one. When you hold up the card, keep your first finger behind it—hidden from the audience. With your other hand, carefully place the glass on top of the card and on the tip of your finger. Your finger will keep the glass from falling. But to the audience, it will look like magic!

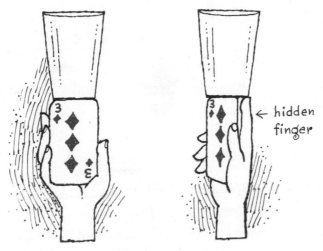

← hidden finger

THE KNOTTY HANDKERCHIEFS ────────★

Three handkerchiefs knot themselves together.

The Trick:

Show three handkerchiefs and place them on a table before you. With your left hand, pick up the handkerchiefs —one by one—and pass them into your right hand.*

* Note: The directions in this book are addressed to right-handed magicians. If you are left-handed substitute "left" for "right" and vice versa.

"Here are three handkerchiefs—a red one, a blue one, and a white one." Roll the handkerchiefs into a ball and throw them into the air. *"Alakazzam!"* They are knotted together!

Materials Needed:
three handkerchiefs
a small rubber band

Before the Show:
Double the rubber band tightly around your right thumb and first two fingers.

Onstage:
As you pass each handkerchief into your right hand, tuck one end inside the rubber band. Slip the rubber band off of your fingers and over the ends of the hand-

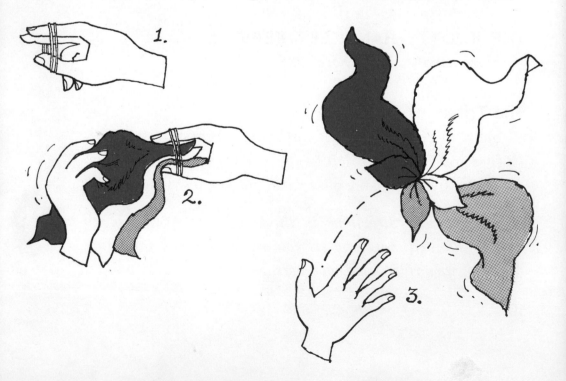

kerchiefs as you roll them into a ball. When you throw them into the air they will look as if they are knotted together.

Tip: Do this trick first on your program. Have the rubber band around your thumb and fingers when you come on stage.

THE PHANTOM DIME ⎯⎯⎯⎯⎯⎯⎯⎯⎯⎯⎯⎯⎯★

A dime vanishes from a paper cup—
then reappears in the magician's pocket.

The Trick:

Drop a dime in a paper cup and cover the cup with a handkerchief. Shake the cup. Everyone can hear the dime inside. *"Abra-ca-da-bra!"* Remove the handkerchief. The cup is empty! Where is the dime? It's in your pocket!

Materials Needed:

a dime
a handkerchief
a paper cup
scissors

Before the Show:

Cut a thin slot near the bottom of the cup.

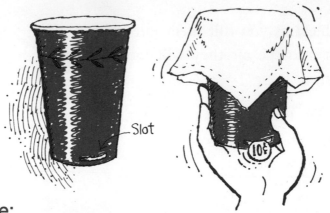

Slot

Onstage:

When you shake the cup, the dime will slide into your hand. Take the cup in your other hand as you say the magic words. While everyone is watching the cup, drop the dime in your pocket. Then whisk away the handkerchief and show the audience the cup is empty. Slowly draw the "phantom" dime from your pocket. Hold it high and take a bow!

THE SPOOKY MATCHBOX ────────────────────────★

A handkerchief appears in an empty box.

The Trick:

Hold up a large matchbox. The drawer is open. Everyone can see it is empty. Close the drawer. Wave your hand over the box. Open the drawer and—*Presto!*—pull out a handkerchief.

Materials Needed:

a large matchbox (the size wooden
 kitchen matches come in)
a handkerchief
scissors

Before the Show:

Take an empty matchbox and remove the drawer from its cover. Cut two slits down the corners of one end of the drawer. Roll a handkerchief into a ball and hide it inside the cover. Then set the drawer just inside the cover in front of the handkerchief (the end with the slits goes in first).

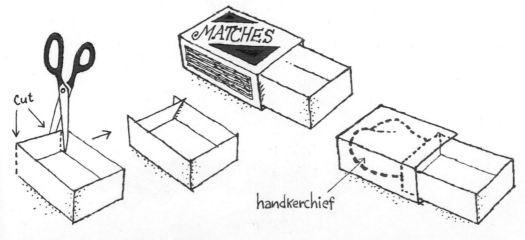

handkerchief

Onstage:

Hold the box in your left hand. Keep the back of the box towards you, so that no one will see the hidden handkerchief. Close the drawer with your right hand. At the same time secretly insert your left first finger into the back of

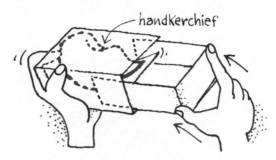

the cover and press it against the handkerchief. The end of the drawer (with the slits) will bend forward and the handkerchief will be forced inside. Wave your hand, open the drawer and pull out the handkerchief to thunderous applause!

THE MAGIC WAND AND THE MAGIC HAT

A top hat and a magic wand are a magician's favorite props. They are easy to make and you can use them to do many mystifying tricks.

HOW TO MAKE A MAGIC WAND ————————————★

Materials Needed:

a wooden dowel, ½ inch in diameter and about 11 inches long (Wooden dowels are available in most hardware stores; or you can cut one from a wooden clothes hanger. Some hangers even have a removable dowel.)

sandpaper

black and white poster paint

Sand the dowel until it is smooth. Then paint the center black. Paint white tips at each end.

Here are some tricks that you can do with your wand.

THE MAGNETIC WAND ————————————————★

The wand sticks to the magician's hand.

The Trick:

Grasp your wand in your left hand. Hold your hand up high. Steady it with your right hand like this. "My wand has magic powers which I will show you." Command the wand to stick to your hand. Slowly open up your thumb and fingers. Nothing is holding the wand, but it doesn't move. Command the wand to move slowly up and down. It does. Now command the wand to fall—and it falls.

How to Do It:

The first finger of your right hand holds the wand in place—or moves it up and down—until you command it to fall.

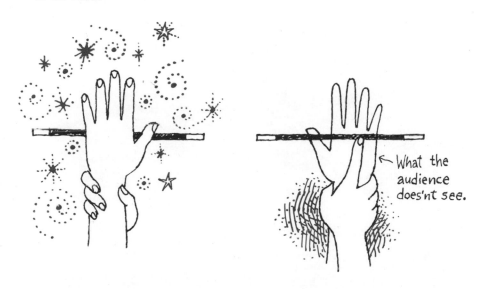

← What the audience does'nt see.

THE VANISHING WAND ————————————————★

The magician's wand disappears—then reappears again.

The Trick:

Hold up your magic wand, then roll it up in a sheet of newspaper. *"Hokus Pokus . . . Pokus Hokus!"* Tear the newspaper in half. The wand has disappeared. Where has it gone? Reach behind you and there it is!

Materials Needed:

a sheet of white paper (about 8½ x 11 inches)
white glue (such as Elmer's Glue-All)
black poster paint

Before the Show:

The vanishing wand is really made of paper. This is how to make it: Roll up a sheet of paper into a tube about the size of your real wand and glue it in place. Paint the center black to look like your real wand. Hide your real wand behind you in a back pocket or inside your sash.

Onstage:

When you tear the newspaper, you'll tear the paper wand, too. Everyone will think that the wand has disappeared. Then bring out the real wand from behind your back. Surprise!

1.

2.

Tip: It is a good idea to make several paper wands at one time. Then you will always have one ready when you need it.

THE RISING WAND ———————————————★

A wand rises and falls in a bottle.

The Trick:

Put your wand into a pop bottle. Command it to rise and it rises! Command it to fall and it falls! Wave your hand over the wand. Walk around the stage. The wand continues to rise and fall whenever you tell it to.

Materials Needed:

a white thumbtack
a spool of black thread
a tinted cola bottle
your magic wand

Before the Show:

Stick a thumbtack into one end of the wand. Tie one end of the black thread around it.

Onstage:

When you put the wand in the bottle, the end with the thread attached goes in first. No one will see the thread because it is dark and very thin. You will need a friend offstage to help you. Your friend will secretly pull on the other end of the thread to make the wand rise and fall, at your command.

HOW TO MAKE A MAGIC HAT————————➤

Materials Needed:
    an empty Quaker Oats box (42 oz. size). (Quaker has
      an unvarnished label paint will stick to.)
    stiff cardboard
    scissors
    white glue (such as Elmer's Glue-All)
    black poster paint
    Before you begin, cut 4 inches off the top of the box.
    The box should then be about 5½ inches high.

Step 1. Make tabs at top of box by cutting slits ¾ inch long and ½ inch apart all around the rim.

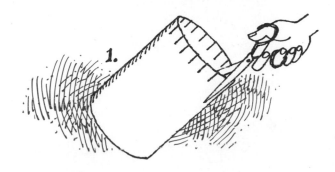

Step 2. Fold tabs out.

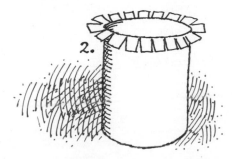

Step 3. Draw a circle 9 inches in diameter on stiff cardboard and cut it out. Set box in center of this circle. Trace around it to make a smaller circle and cut it out. You now have a cardboard brim.

9 inches

Cut out

Step 4. Turn the box upside down and slip brim down over bottom of box and glue it to the tabs.

—Put glue on tabs.

Step 5. Make another brim by repeating Step #3. With box right-side up, spread glue on top of first brim. Glue second brim to it to cover tabs.

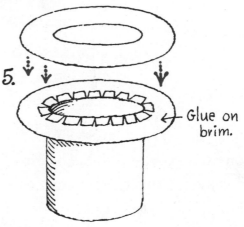

← Glue on brim.

Step 6. Paint hat black inside and out.

THE RABBIT IN THE HAT ———————————————————⋆

The magician's hat looks empty—but not for long!

The Trick:

Hold up your magic hat. Everyone can see inside. It looks empty. Wave your magic wand. *"Hokus Pokus—Dom-i-nocus!"* Reach into the hat and pull out a rabbit.

Materials Needed:

your magic hat

a round piece of black cloth—a little larger
than the bottom of your hat

a toy rabbit (You can make one easily.
The directions follow on pages 34–36.)

How to Do It:

The rabbit is in the hat all the time. It is folded neatly in the bottom and covered with the black cloth. The cloth will look like the bottom of the hat, and the hat will appear to be empty. When you reach into the hat, push the cloth to one side and bring out the rabbit. Just for fun hide a carrot in the hat, too. Pull it out and offer it to the rabbit.

← Cloth to cover rabbit

Rabbit folded inside hat.

Materials Needed:

One white cotton tube sock (a sock that doesn't
   have a shaped heel and toe)
paper towels for stuffing
15 inches of red ribbon, ½ inch wide
tracing paper
a 4 x 6 inch piece of white felt
a 7 inch square of black cloth
felt-tipped pens—pink and black
one small safety pin
one rubber band
one cotton ball
scissors
white glue (such as Elmer's Glue-All)

Step 1. Lay tube sock flat on table. Note location of
seam.

Step 2. Squeeze paper towel into shape of small lemon.
Stuff into toe of sock to form rabbit's head. Double a
rubber band around sock to shape rabbit's neck.

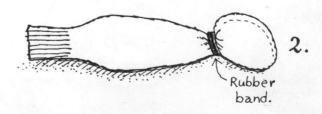

Step 3. Roll up top of sock and tuck inside body. Stuff more paper toweling into body to round it out. Glue cotton ball to back for a tail.

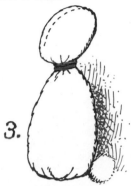

Step 4. To make rabbit's ears, trace the pattern on page 36, and cut it out. Tape or pin it to two layers of felt and carefully cut around it. Glue ears to each side of rabbit's head, as shown.

Step 5. Draw a face with felt-tipped pens. Make nose and eyeballs pink. Outline eyes and mouth with black. Draw thin black whiskers.

Step 6. Tie ribbon around neck and make a bow. Use black cloth to make a cape, just like yours. Wrap it around rabbit's shoulders and pin it in front.

6.

←Pattern for
   Rabbit's ears.

TRICKIER TRICKS: YOUR FRIENDS HAVE FUN, TOO!

For these tricks you'll need a helper—sometimes, two. Choose them from the audience. Be careful—don't let them learn your secrets. You'll want to fool them, too!

THE MAGIC WATER TRICK ————————————★

The magician makes water flow from a volunteer's elbow.

The Trick:

Hold up a glass of water. "This is magic water. Anyone who drinks it will become rich and famous." Ask if anyone in the audience would like to drink it. A brave volunteer steps up to the stage and drinks the water. Wait for a few seconds; then pretend to be very upset. "Oh, no!

I've given you the wrong glass! *That* water will make you grow ten feet tall! We must do something fast before it starts to work!" Quickly roll up the volunteer's sleeve, bend his arm forward, and place a funnel under his elbow.

Next ask someone in the audience to help you. Tell your helper to move the volunteer's other arm up and down like a pump handle. Then, to everyone's amazement, the magic water flows through the funnel into a glass below.

Materials Needed:
a piece of sponge (about 2 inches square)
a small metal kitchen funnel
a glass
waterproof glue (such as Duco Cement)

Before the Show:
Glue the sponge to the inside of the funnel. Let the glue dry, then wet the sponge. Hold the funnel over the sink until the sponge stops dripping. Then set the funnel upside down on your table, to have ready for the show.

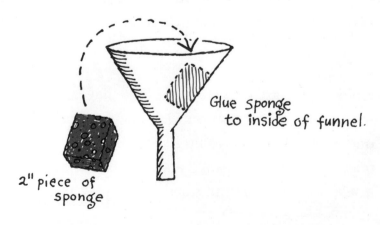

Glue sponge to inside of funnel.

2" piece of sponge

Onstage:

When you pick up the funnel, cover the sponge with your fingers. No one will know the sponge is there. Hold the funnel under the volunteer's elbow. As your helper pumps the volunteer's arm, press your fingers against the wet sponge and the water will come out of the funnel. Hold a glass in your other hand to catch it.

THE CHANGING BAG ⎯⎯⎯⎯⎯⎯⎯⎯⎯⎯⎯⎯⎯★

A white napkin changes into a red one.

The Trick:

Show a paper bag. Let everyone see inside. It looks empty. Put a white napkin in the bag. Wave the bag in the air.

"Shazzim—Shazzam!" Ask someone from the audience to reach in the bag. Is the napkin still there? Yes, but it has changed color. Now it's red!

Materials Needed:

two brown notion bags—about 7½ x 10 inches
   (This is the type of bag that you get
   in the drug store or variety store.)
two small paper napkins—one red and one white
white glue (such as Elmer's Glue-All)
scissors

Before the Show:

The changing bag is really two bags that are glued together to look like one. This is how to make it: Cut across the top of each bag to make the edges even (Figure 1). Then glue the bags together back to back, first turning one bag upside down (Figure 2). When the glue is dry, put the red napkin into one of the bags.

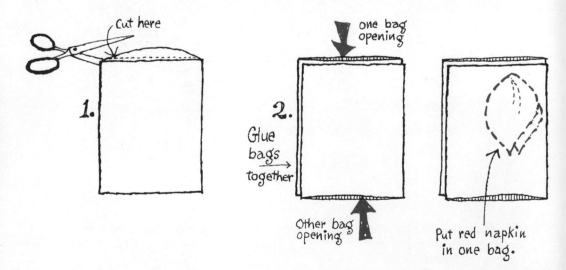

Onstage:

Show the audience the inside of the other bag—the empty one. Tuck the white napkin into it and wave the bag in the air. As you do this, secretly turn the bag upside down. Then ask someone to reach into the opening that's now facing up, and they will pull out the hidden red napkin.

Tip: When you turn the bags upside down, the napkins might fall out if you're not careful. To keep that from happening, unfold each napkin first. Stuff it loosely into the bag and push it down to the bottom. It will stay there until you pull it out.

THE BROKEN MATCH MYSTERY ———————✶

A broken match becomes whole again!

The Trick:

Hold up a handkerchief and a wooden match. Wrap the match in the handkerchief. Ask a volunteer from the audience to hold the match through the handkerchief. "Do you feel the match?" The volunteer answers, "Yes." "Now break the match in half." SNAP! The match is broken. *"Abra-ca-da-bra!"* Shake the handkerchief. The match falls out—but it is whole again!

Materials Needed:

2 wooden matches
a handkerchief

41

Before the Show:

Use a handkerchief with a wide hem. Cut open the hem at one corner and slip a match into it until it is hidden. If you don't have a handkerchief with a hem, fold back a corner edge just enough to cover the match and sew it neatly in place.

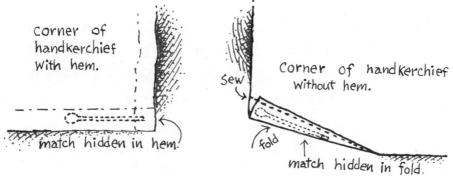

corner of handkerchief with hem.

match hidden in hem.

Sew

Corner of handkerchief without hem.

fold

match hidden in fold.

Onstage:

Open the handkerchief and place it on the palm of your left hand. With your right hand, show the duplicate match and place it in the center of the handkerchief. Then fold each corner of the handkerchief toward the center to cover it. Fold the corner that contains the hidden match last and hold on to it with your right hand. Allow the volunteer to feel the hidden match and ask him to break it.

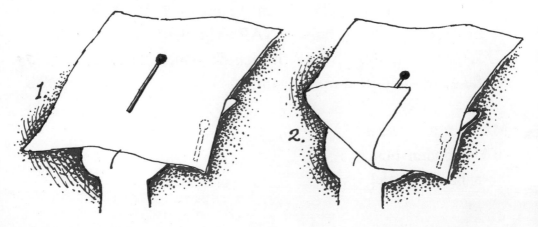

1.

2.

(Meanwhile keep the duplicate match tucked safely in the bottom of the handkerchief, inside your left palm.) After the match has been broken, shake the handkerchief. The broken match will stay inside the hem and only the unbroken one will fall out.

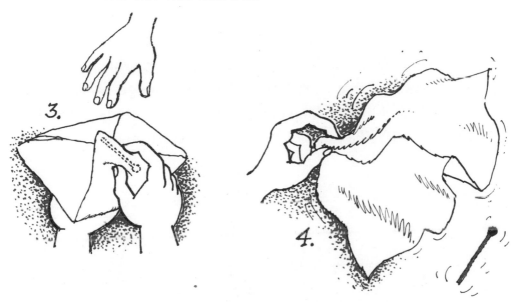

THE LOOP AND CORD MYSTERY ————————✶

A paper loop passes through a piece of cord.

The Trick:

Choose a spectator from the audience to help you. Hand him (or her) a piece of cord. Ask him to tie one end around each of your wrists, leaving some cord between them. Show everyone a paper loop. Then turn your back for a few seconds. *"Abra-ca-da-bra! Ala-kaz-zam!"* When you turn around the loop is hanging on the cord.

Materials Needed:

two strips of heavy paper (each 1 x 10 inches)
white glue (such as Elmer's Glue-All)
a 3 foot cord

Before the Show:

There are really two loops that look exactly the same. Make them from the strips of heavy paper. Glue the ends together so that each loop is just big enough to fit over your fist. Slip one loop onto your wrist. Double it around your wrist like this (Figure 1) and hide it under the cuff of your sleeve.

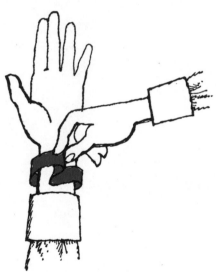

Onstage:

Show the audience the other loop. As soon as your back is turned, tuck this loop into your shirt pocket, or inside your sash. Then slip the hidden loop over your hand and onto the cord.

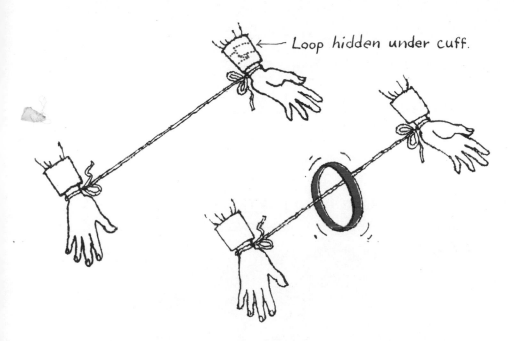

← Loop hidden under cuff.

Tip: The loops must be heavy enough so that they will not tear easily. For a good strong loop, cut the strips from a heavy grocery bag. You can paint them a bright color so they can be easily seen by the audience.

MYSTIFYING TRICKS THAT MAY FOOL YOU, TOO!

These tricks are fun to do. They almost work by themselves. Just follow the directions and you'll surprise your friends every time. You may even be surprised, too!

THE INVISIBLE PENNY ————————————★

A penny disappears under a glass of water.

Materials Needed:

a clear drinking glass or a glass jar
a sheet of paper (about 8½ x 11 inches)
a penny
tape and crayons

Before the Show:

With crayons, color the paper red or black. (Don't use colored construction paper as it tears too easily.) Decorate it with gold or silver stars. Then wrap the paper loosely around the glass and tape it in place. Twist the top to close it. This makes a paper cover. Fill the glass with water and set it on the table, to have ready for the show.

Onstage:

Show the glass of water and place the paper cover over it. Show the penny, and set it on the table. Cover it with the glass. *"Hokus Pokus. . . . Pokus Hokus!"* Lift the paper cover halfway up the glass. The penny is gone! Lower the cover and wave your hands. Lift up the glass and there is the penny!

Why it Works:

The penny is there all the time. You can't see it because the glass is full of water. The water bends the light's rays so that you can't see what's underneath the glass.

Tip: Do this trick on a low table or stool so that the audience can easily see the bottom of the glass. Cover the table with a white cloth. The penny will show up better (before it disappears!)

THE FUNNY PAPER LOOPS —————————————★

The magician cuts a paper loop and funny things happen.

The Trick:

Show a large paper loop and cut it along the center line (Figure 1). When you are finished cutting you should have two loops, but you don't. Instead you have one large loop. Try again! Cut the large loop along the center line (Figure 2). Success! This time you have two loops, but something strange has happened. One loop is twisted around the other!

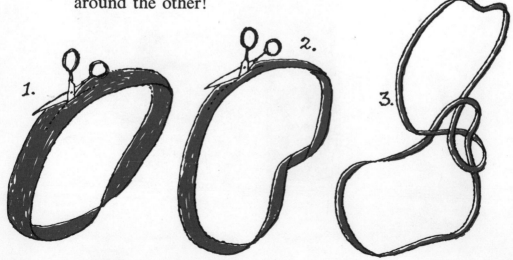

Materials Needed:
a sheet of newspaper
scissors
white glue (such as Elmer's Glue-All)

Before the Show:
Cut two strips of newspaper—each about 4 inches wide and 2 feet long. Glue the ends together to make one long strip (about 4 feet long).

Glue together

Now spread glue along the top of the strip and along the bottom. Then join the ends to make a loop, but first give one end a half turn so that the glued ends come together. This is called a Möbius strip. Scientists and mathematicians as well as magicians know it behaves in weird ways. Just start cutting it and see how funny it can be!

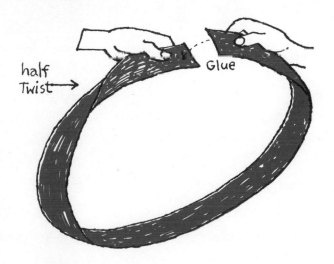

half
Twist →   Glue

THE IMPOSSIBLE TRICK ━━━━━━━━━━━━━━━━━━━━★

A postcard fits over the magician's head.

The Trick:

Hold up a postcard and a scissors. Tell everyone that you
are going to do the impossible. "I am going to cut this
card in such a way that it will fit over my head." Everyone will say that it can't be done. SNIP! SNIP! "Just
watch and see."

Materials Needed:

a postcard or file card
scissors (a short pair is best)

How to Do it:

Fold the card in half lengthwise. At the folded edge, cut
7 slits evenly across it. This is easy to do if you make

the slits in the order shown in the drawing (Figure 1). Do not cut all the way through.

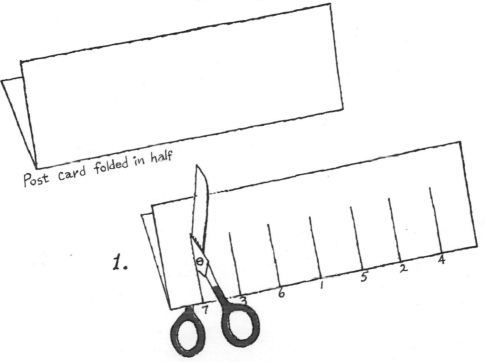

Post card folded in half

1.

Turn the card around. From the outer edge, cut a slit between each of the first slits (6 in all). Cut close to the fold but do not cut through it (Figure 2).

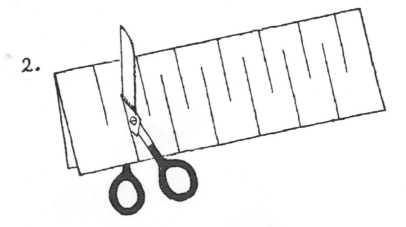

2.

Now turn the card around again and cut along the fold but *only* where you see the dotted lines (Figure 3). (Be careful not to cut into the second set of slits.)

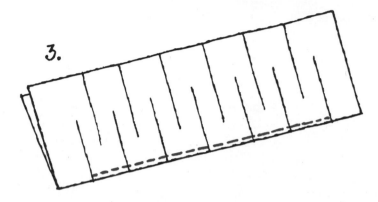

3.

Unfold the card carefully and slip it over your head. The "impossible" has been done!

BIG TRICKS
FOR THE GRAND FINALE

These tricks are hard acts to follow, so save them for the
end.

THE MAGIC CONE ———————————————————★
Ribbons, cards and bright scarves appear in an empty cone.

The Trick:

Hold up a newspaper. Show both sides to the audience,
then roll it into a cone. *"Hokus Pokus . . . Pokus
Hokus!"* Reach into the cone. Pull out scarves, playing
cards and bright silk ribbons.

Materials Needed:

newspaper
white glue (such as Elmer's Glue-All)
one or two small silk scarves
ribbons
playing cards

Before the Show:

The newspaper has a secret pocket in it. This is how to prepare it: Use a double sheet of newspaper. Fold and glue the sheet together so that a pocket is formed at one side. The dotted lines will show you where to spread the glue (Figure 1). Allow the glue to dry. Then hide the cards, ribbons and scarves neatly inside the pocket.

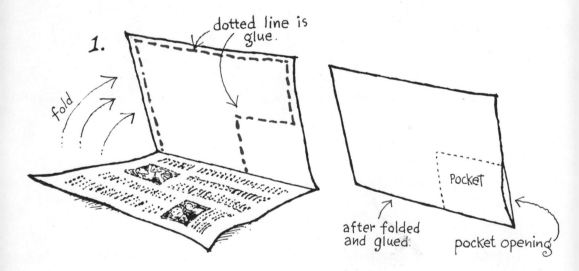

1.

fold

dotted line is glue.

after folded and glued.

Pocket

pocket opening

Onstage:

Keep your hand over the pocket opening when you hold up the newspaper. Show the newspaper on both sides and roll it into a cone. This is how to do it: Fold the corner with the pocket towards the center of the sheet (Figure 2). Then wrap the other side of the paper around it (Figure 3). The pocket opening will then be inside the cone near the top (Figure 4). Reach into the pocket and surprise everyone.

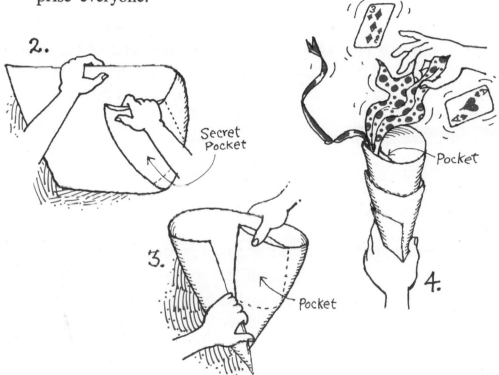

2.

Secret
Pocket

Pocket

3.

Pocket

4.

NOW YOU SEE ME—NOW YOU DON'T! ⎯⎯→⋆
The magician vanishes into thin air!

The Trick:

Hold up a large sheet in front of you. No one can see you behind the sheet. Suddenly the sheet drops to the floor, and you are gone!

Materials Needed:
    a sheet
    a yardstick
    needle and thread

Before the Show:
Sew a large hem in the top of the sheet. Insert a yardstick into the hem (Figure 1). Sew up each end of the hem so the yardstick won't slip out.

1.

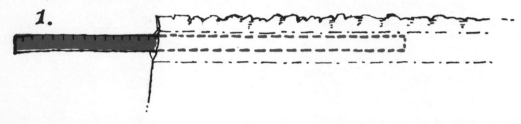

Onstage:
Stand just beside a doorway or a partially opened curtain. Raise the sheet in front of you—the bottom should touch the floor so the audience can no longer see you. Hold on to the yardstick with both hands (Figure 2).

2.

curtain or doorframe

Sheet

Now let go with one hand, so you can move behind the doorway. Continue holding the yardstick up with your other hand (Figure 3). Everyone will think that you are still behind the sheet.

Then pull this hand back quickly and let the sheet fall (Figure 4). Make a quick get-a-way, if possible, to be truly mystifying. Or come suddenly back on stage to make your grand finale bow!

NOW YOU'RE A MAGICIAN: HOW TO BE A BETTER ONE

Here are some important rules that all magicians follow.

Never tell how a trick is done. Magicians never tell their secrets. It spoils the fun.

Never tell the audience what is going to happen next. Keep them guessing. Then you can take them by surprise and fool them.

Don't repeat a trick before the same audience. They might catch on the second time and figure out your secret.

Watch other magicians perform. Study how they move and what they say. Use their ideas to make your own show a better one.

If you see another magician doing a trick that you know, be polite and act surprised. Don't give the trick away.

Practice each trick over and over again until you can do it well. Practice what you will say with each trick. That's important, too. Practice is *the* magic word. Without it, your tricks will probably fail.

Be a showman, not a showoff. Laugh at yourself, but never at the audience. Remember you are fooling them because you like them and want them to have a good time. That's what makes giving a magic show so much fun.

METRIC CONVERSION CHART

1 inch	= 2.54 centimeters or 25.4 millimeters
1 foot	= 0.30 meters
1 yard	= 0.91 meters

1 millimeter	= 0.04 inches
1 centimeter	= 0.39 inches
1 meter	= 39.37 inches, 3.3 feet, or 1.1 yards

The measurements used in this book are inches and feet. To convert to the metric system, round off the numbers as outlined in the following chart.

¼ inch	= 6 mm	4 inches	= 10 cm
½ inch	= 1.25 cm	10 inches	= 25 cm
1 inch	= 2.50 cm	1 foot	= 30 cm
2 inches	= 5 cm	2 feet	= 60 cm
3 inches	= 7.50 cm	3 feet	= 90 cm

INDEX TO THE TRICKS

INDEX

(See also Index to the Tricks, page 61)